MAN FAIL

Stupid Things Men Do

MARION APPLEBY

Michael O'Mara Books Limited

First published in Great Britain in 2012 by
Michael O'Mara Books Limited
9 Lion Yard
Tremadoc Road
London SW4 7NQ

A CIP catalogue record for this book is available from the British Library.

Papers used by Michael O'Mara Books Limited are natural, recyclable products made from wood grown in sustainable forests. The manufacturing processes conform to the environmental regulations of the country of origin.

ISBN: 978-1-84317-698-5 in paperback print format
ISBN 978-1-84317-985-6 in EPub format
ISBN 978-1-84317-986-3 in Mobipocket format

1 2 3 4 5 6 7 8 9 10

Illustrations by Andrew Pinder

Printed and bound in Great Britain by Cox and Wyman

www.mombooks.com

Contents

Contents

INTRODUCTION

The Simpler Sex

Somebody terribly clever once said that it was human to err. By 'err' they did of course mean 'fail', and by 'humans' they did in fact mean 'men' – as will become clear as you read this book. And read it you must, men, not least to feel better about yourselves. Because you cannot possibly be as thoughtless as the Russian man who forfeited his wife during a game of cards; as hapless as the hopeless man who was shot by his own dog; or as daft as the dimwit who impaled himself through the eyeball on his own secateurs. So read this book, men, read it, puff out your chests and be thankful that you are not them.

As for the female readership: consider this book a warning – there are some very silly men out there, and they know not what they're doing. You don't want to marry a man who thinks it's sensible to get a tattoo that runs down the length of his penis; you definitely don't want to end up dating the sort of man who accidentally nails himself to the wall with a power tool during a spot of DIY; and you certainly don't want to wake up next to a chap who prefers to do his weekly food shop without any shoes on.

No. You can do better than this, so use this book as a handy guide. After reading it, you should be able to spot them from a mile off.

ROMANCE

FAIL

Stupid Cupids

Men generally aren't the most romantic of souls, but some chaps really do take the biscuit, as we'll see in the following pages. Goodness knows what possessed one dumb dope to think pinching a stranger on the bottom was a viable substitute for a 'How d'ya do?', or why another lovesick fool thought it wise to bury his prospective (and, it seemed, very hungry) fiancée's engagement ring inside a muffin . . .

For Better or . . . Nah, Forget It

Grooms, be warned – what happens in Vegas doesn't always stay in Vegas, as one foolish reveller found out when he 'dabbled' on his stag weekend in Sin City. Having 'hooked up' with a lady to whom he was not betrothed, the blundering idiot then failed to cover his tracks, leaving incriminating texts on his mobile phone for his (lawyer) fiancée to find on his return. He decided to cancel the wedding, for which his bride-to-be had paid in full; she then decided to sue him for the entire cost of the ceremony, which came to a rather unromantic total of $62,814.

Cheeky Boy

If you must indulge in some bottom-pinching, it's best to make sure that it's a) someone you know, and b) not a policewoman. Sadly this didn't stop Englishman

Bradley Richards from giving Police Community Support Officer Claire Jones a quick nip on the arse after asking for her number. His sentence for common assault suggests she wasn't so forthcoming.

With This Muffin I Thee Wed

Calling all would-be proposers – think long and hard before you hide the engagement ring in your future fiancée's food. One poor Chinese chap learned the hard way when he hid a ring worth £500 in a muffin … and his girlfriend promptly ate the whole thing. Doctors had to perform endoscopic surgery to remove the bling. Said the romantic fool, 'I'm not sure she will ever feel very comfortable wearing it, even though I spent hours cleaning it for her.'

First-Date Jitters?

A first date in North Carolina came to an abrupt end when the man somehow shot himself in the leg. Putting paid to any plans he might have had for coffee, the unfortunate chap managed to shoot himself after laying his hands on a gun located underneath his car seat as he prepared to drive his date home. Police ruled that the shooting was accidental, although they sadly failed to confirm whether the unlucky couple made it to a second date.

Sibling Rivalry

The groom at a wedding in India arrived at his own nuptials so intoxicated the bride refused to marry him. Proceedings, however, didn't end in total disaster, as the bride decided to marry the groom's (younger, more sober) brother instead. Although the intended groom apologized for his behaviour, his pleas were ignored and he was reported to have been seen crying and wailing about how he would never find another woman to marry him.

Apple of His Eye

A man in Zimbabwe was forced to serve up a whole tray of humble pie when he called a prostitute to his hotel room and opened the door to . . . his daughter. He collapsed to the floor in shock, his daughter bolted, and his wife admitted to newspaper reporters that their marriage was 'troubled'.

FAIL

'The Internet is a great way to get on the Net.'

Bob Dole, one-time Republican presidential candidate

Target Practice

Chivalry may not be dead, but, chaps, you might want to think twice before agreeing to carry your girlfriend's gun. After offering to take care of his fiancée's pink pistol during a trip to the supermarket, Joshua Seto experienced some difficulty securing the firearm and promptly shot himself in the crown jewels. According to reports, 'It was unclear whether he suffered any permanent damage from the incident.'

Baby Rage

Although your first-born can induce a fair degree of stress, most don't act as expectant father Charlie Humphreys from Bristol did. While driving his girlfriend to hospital, where she was due to give birth, the miscreant found himself embroiled in a road-rage incident that led him to punch a stranger repeatedly in the face. After a rather bizarre mix-up in which Humphreys mistakenly thought a car horn was being honked at him, he decided to leave his vehicle and assault another driver. Worse still, while he was doing so, one of his fellow passengers stole the victim's car. Humphreys was sentenced to 200 hours of community service.

Sorry Sandwich

A cheating boyfriend took drastic steps to try to win back his girlfriend when he paraded around the centre of Brighton wearing a sandwich board that declared his guilt. With 'I cheated on my girlfriend. I am humiliating myself to show I am sorry' emblazoned on the front, and 'I love her so much. I will do anything to get her back. I am sorry' on the back, the chap perplexed shoppers, who were divided as to whether his stunt classified as 'romantic' or 'horrifying'. Amazingly his girlfriend reluctantly agreed to take him back … as long as he slept on the sofa.

FAIL

'People hate me because I am a multifaceted, talented, wealthy, internationally famous genius.'

Jerry Lewis, humanitarian and comedian

Place Your Bets

It's generally advised that a person should not bet more than he can afford to lose, a rule Andrei Karpov of Russia flounced when he put up his own wife as a stake during a card game. Unfortunately he lost, and when his opponen, Sergey Brodov, later arrived to claim his winnings, Karpov's wife was reportedly so angry she decided to divorce her husband. In a fitting, if slightly strange, twist, she chose Brodov as her second husband. 'I am very happy with him,' she said. 'Even if he did "win" me in a poker game.'

FAIL

'It's the sort of vague calm you get after vomiting . . . where the vomit itself is rather unpleasant, but when it's over, it brings a kind of strange peace.'

Ben Affleck describes the nausea he felt after breaking up with Jennifer Lopez

What an Ass

While some of us may have experienced the occasional drunken blackout, be very thankful you've never found yourself in the same position as the Zimbabwean chap who woke up one Sunday morning after a night out drinking to find himself accused of having had sex with a donkey. Struggling to remember the events of the fateful evening, the man later told the court that he had in fact paid for the services of a prostitute, but he wasn't aware the prostitute had transformed into a donkey. 'I do not know what happened when I left the bar,' he admitted, 'but I am seriously in love with [the] donkey.'

*'I owe a lot to my parents, especially my
mother and father.'*

Greg Norman, Australian golfer

A Woman in Every Town

A woman in Michigan discovered her husband had found himself a second wife after she came across his new wedding photos on a mutual friend's Facebook page. Police investigations discovered that the man had married his first wife while absconding from parole and had consequently been sent back to prison. It was while on release from this second term, when he was no longer living near his first wife, that he met and married his second wife. The greedy fellow must have had a hell of a lot of stamina . . .

Naked Nuptials

A wedding in Austria ended in disaster when the groom was caught having sex with a waitress at his own wedding reception. As if to make matters worse, the dastardly dingbat was caught in the act by his brand-new father-in-law, who immediately ordered the guests to leave. Unfortunately the poor bride had to wait six months before she could divorce her philandering husband in accordance with Austrian law.

FAIL

'The Beatles? They're on the wane.'

Prince Philip in 1965

What a Riot!

In 2012 a wedding in Boston, Massachusetts, ended in a lot of tears when a fight broke out during the reception. It all began when the groom's underage brothers were refused alcohol at the reception's bar. In protest, the groom got very angry and started kicking and punching the walls; he got even angrier when a member of the bride's family tried to intervene to calm him down. Obviously the chap was cut from the same cloth as his mother, because she too got in on the action, attacking the bride's mum. The day ended with the arrest of – you guessed it – the groom's mother *and* the girlfriend of one of the groom's younger brothers.

On the Head!

In June 2012 Newcastle United football player Danny Guthrie's nuptials erupted into violence after a food fight began at his wedding reception. The opulent day, which cost a grand total of £40,000 to produce, began well but soon turned sour when the lobster thermidor was flung about with gay abandon. All light-hearted fun, one might think, until the poor bride was walloped in the face by one of the guests. 'They [the guests] were obnoxious and disgusting,' said a witness to the day's events.

Cold Feet

In 2008 a silly chap in Japan went about cancelling his impending nuptials in completely the wrong way. Despite the fact that he already had a wife, Tatsuhiko Kawata got engaged to another lady ... but come the day of the wedding, he was having second thoughts. Rather than cancelling the planned event in an adult fashion, Kawata decided instead to sabotage the nuptials by setting fire to the hotel where the ceremony was due to take place. He was promptly arrested and sent to prison.

FAIL

'China is a big country, inhabited by many Chinese.'

Former French president, and all-round bright spark, Charles de Gaulle

Popping the Question

In 2008 born-romantic Lefkos Hajji from London decided to ask his girlfriend to marry him by hiding a £6,000 diamond ring in a balloon. No sooner had Hajji asked a florist to place the ring in a helium balloon than a gust of wind blew the balloon away, taking the very expensive ring with it. Hajji tried in vain to catch up with the floating cargo, chasing it in his car for almost two hours. He should have listened to the florist, who was reported to have said, 'I thought he was taking a risk. I said, "I hope you hold on to it."'

For Better, for Worse

Devoted husband Alan Jenkins decided to have life-sized portraits of his wife and children tattooed onto his back as a demonstration of his lifelong commitment to them. Unfortunately no sooner had the twenty-hour-long procedure been completed than Jenkins discovered his wife had been cheating on him with a fitness instructor. She could have at least told him about the affair before he got her face etched onto his back!

FAIL

'Ghastly.'

Prince Philip's description of Beijing during a royal visit to China in 1986

Flash the Cash

In 2009 a man in China was arrested after he tried to deposit a cheque worth $36.5 million into his bank account. The cheque was, of course, a fake, and the man was almost immediately arrested. Upon confrontation, the silly thing admitted he'd thought the massive wedge of cash might impress a woman who'd been present while he tried to pay the money in. A bunch of flowers would have sufficed!

FAIL

'I used to be the future president of the United States.'

Al Gore

Russian Roulette

A wedding in Russia in 2010 ended in disaster when a prank pulled by one of the guests went seriously wrong. A friend of the groom decided to play what he thought was a fake game of Russian roulette. He pulled a gun from his waistband, pointed it straight at his own head and pulled the trigger. The gun fired a blank, which led another wedding guest to try the trick for himself. But after pulling the trigger, the second man fell immediately to the floor . . . It turned out the gun had fired a rubber bullet at point-blank range directly into his skull. The gunman's claim that he'd emptied the gun of all bullets seemed a somewhat unlikely story.

FAIL

'Facts are stupid things.'

Ronald Reagan

Foolish Felons

It's an unfortunate statistic, but accurate: historically the majority of crimes have been carried out by men, so you'd think they might be better at it by now. However, as the following tales of crap criminals, hapless hoodlums and bungling burglars will attest, the answer to that is, apparently not.

Sausage Fingers

A fumbling Frenchman was convicted of driving under the influence of alcohol after he accidentally mixed up the phone numbers of the local gendarmes and his vehicle breakdown service. While the silly fool was six times over the limit, his car went kaput in the middle of nowhere, leaving him drunkenly stranded. Reaching for his mobile phone, he called what he thought was the breakdown service – but was in fact the local cops – telling the operator who answered that they should come quickly because he was very squiffy and didn't want to get picked up by the police. Oops!

Not So Crafty

Englishman Ryan Crafts was arrested after he left behind some rather incriminating evidence having burgled a house while the owners slept. Upon waking and discovering that a laptop, an iPod and a set of car keys had gone walkies, the poor victims saw that their mobile phones were missing too. Luckily for them, the not-so-bright burglar had left behind his own phone, allowing police to quickly locate its owner – the hapless Crafts.

Put the Pen Down!

In the USA two clueless nitwits decided to do away with the traditional method of a mask disguise when they set out to rob an apartment. Instead, they chose to use a black marker pen to scribble on their faces.

A few problems arose: one, the pen was running out; two, they only scrawled on a bit of their faces; three, you could still see EXACTLY WHAT THEY LOOKED LIKE. The pitiful pair were, of course, very easy to track down, whereupon they were charged with second-degree burglary.

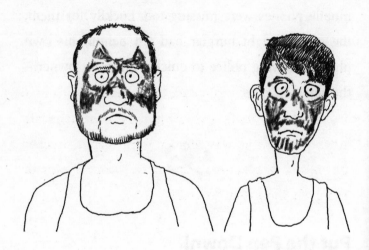

Artless

A would-be art thief left behind a trail of clues when he splattered half a pint of his own blood and left a multitude of fingerprints at the crime scene. Breaking the window of a Brooklyn restaurant, the thief intended to steal one of the New York eatery's paintings, but after cutting his hands on the glass, he managed to make off with just one computer. This was not the only bungle he made: having used a fire extinguisher to bash down a door, the crap criminal managed to set it off, covering himself with chemicals. After the culprit was almost immediately tracked down, a police source was said to quip, 'He made more of a mess than anything.'

Fat Chance

The award for 'Most Ridiculous Excuse Ever' goes to the able-bodied bloke caught using a fake disabled parking badge in Manchester, UK. After his first claim that the badge had been issued by a London council fell on deaf ears, he then tried arguing that he had attempted to use a parking meter but the coins wouldn't go in the machine because they were too 'fat'. Chubby coinage – that old chestnut!

The Great Pretender

A man in Mumbai was so desperate to gain respect he posed as a police doctor by placing two red police beacons on top of his car and carrying around with him two walkie-talkies, under the pretence they were police radios. When he was finally arrested by the real police, it also transpired the man had covered his car in police logo stickers.

Fail to Plan

Two rubber-headed thieves broke into a tyre factory in Malaysia, but their failure to plan the crime properly brought proceedings to a swift end. The two chaps had intended to make off with a haul of wheels to sell on for parts, but they managed to forget a few important details – like a getaway car or, say, something to put the tyres in. After trying and failing to gain entry by forcing a lock, the burglars then attempted to hop over the gates, but police in the area saw them behaving suspiciously and promptly arrested them. They were remanded in custody and told to think about what they'd done (or, more appropriately, not done) for a very long time.

Just Not Cricket

The owner of an English cricket club was left perplexed after his beloved clubhouse was broken into but nothing of value was taken. The bungling burglars had spent hours trying to break into the property and, once inside, ransacked the clubhouse, ignored the valuable alcohol and sporting equipment in store there, and instead decided to steal the safe. And two bottles of alcopops. Not only was the safe ridiculously heavy, after managing to roll it to the bottom of a hill, the dim-witted duo found their path was blocked by a water feature, and so spent some time rolling it back up the hill again. Another problem? The safe was empty, which meant that in the end their total haul comprised two bottles of alcopops. As the club's estates manager, quipped, 'The only thing they really got that night was a workout . . . Their faces must have been a picture when they found the safe was empty.'

FAIL

'You know the one thing that's wrong
with this country? Everyone gets a
chance to have their fair say.'

Bill Clinton

Patience Is a Virtue

Brian Butler put civility ahead of criminality when he queued up to rob a petrol station in Sunderland, UK. The patient pilferer was captured on CCTV calmly waiting his turn behind customers lining up to pay for their petrol. And Butler's politeness didn't end there – by the time he reached the front of the queue he quietly handed the cashier a note that rather sinisterly mentioned he had on his person 'a Stanley knife and a hammer'. Unfortunately, while he'd remembered to wear camouflage, he hadn't remembered to pick up the weapons before he left the house. Police were able to identify the hapless stick-up merchant from the security tapes, and he was later sentenced to six years in the slammer.

Barefooted Bozo

A daft burglar in England was caught out when he removed his trainers after entering the property . . . and accidentally left them behind. Although it's possible he took the shoes off out of politeness, it's more likely he was trying to keep quiet while he committed his crime. However, he wasn't quite quiet enough – when the sleeping homeowner awoke, the felon fled the scene, leaving his trainers behind as evidence. Handing down a sentence of two and a half years, Judge Alistair McCreath failed to comment on whether the burglar might want to think about wearing slippers next time.

FAIL

'He's a guy who gets up at six o'clock in the morning, regardless of what time it is.'

Lou Duva, veteran boxing trainer and member of the International Boxing Hall of Fame

Opportunity Knocks

One young opportunist in Florida showed his entrepreneurial side when he asked a stranger he'd mistakenly dialled if he'd like to buy some drugs. Deal done, the daring young fool arranged to meet the customer in a nearby school car park to complete the transaction . . . only to be met by the law – it turns out the number he'd called belonged to a local police officer. You can't blame a guy for trying.

Puppy Love

Potty puppy-lover James Allsopp was so enamoured with his new boxer that he set up a complex CCTV system so he could keep an eye on the mutt while he was out at work. Imagine Allsopp's surprise when, sitting at his desk awaiting doggy updates, he witnessed burglar Ashley Burton breaking into his house. The alarm went off, the police were called and, although Burton had by this point scarpered, he was quickly tracked down due to his distinctive (i.e. bright red) tracksuit.

Worth a Try

Feeling a little empty of pocket? Then why not do as Charles Ray Fuller of Texas did and cash a cheque for $360 billion. Arrested while trying to complete the ambitious transaction, Fuller insisted it was totally above board, and was in fact a gift from his girlfriend's mum to help him start his own record business. When the teller contacted the account holder, Fuller was quickly disabused of this notion and charged with forgery, along with unlawfully carrying a weapon and possession of marijuana.

Mum, Can You Come and Get Me?

Three men phoned the police and asked them to come and quickly, er, arrest them because, after trying to break into a home in the western suburbs of Delhi, they'd suddenly found the house surrounded by

the victim's furious neighbours. The burglars were
scared and clearly thought a few years in the slammer
preferable to a telling-off from some very angry
suburbanites.

Smile! You're on *Candid Camera* . . .

Sometimes even criminals desire fame, which might explain the actions of three, frankly useless, burglars in Florida. Anthony and Joshua VanSlyke and their friend Gregory Williams were arrested after they made a home video that explained exactly how they were going to carry out their next burglary. To help the prosecution's case further, the film contained close-up shots of their faces, and sample dialogue included the killer line 'What are we going to do? We're going to prize off the hinges on the door!' Policemen caught the hapless trio in the act and the video was found in one of their pockets – but by that point they'd presumably gone a bit camera-shy.

Bread Head

A young Australian man decided to break into a bakery via a skylight while waiting for his friends to pick him up after a boozy night out. Just as soon as he was in, the miscreant quickly realized that not only was there nothing to steal, he also couldn't get out. In an attempt to escape, the bungling burglar was caught on CCTV trying to fashion makeshift ladders from buckets of flour and shelving units, but he kept falling over, covering himself in bread-making ingredients in the process. Although he eventually escaped, he was finally tracked down after footage of his misdemeanour was broadcast extensively on news channels. His legal team devised the rather questionable defence that the silly fool's motive for breaking in was because 'He was hungry.'

Domestic

While women might complain that men don't know where the laundry basket is located, Arizona's Michael Trias knew exactly where to find one . . . after he fell and got stuck inside a basket while trying to burgle a house. The clumsy felon was lodged for so long he had to rely on the help of the homeowner to free him. The cops later told the press that while nothing had been taken from the home, there had been damage to the window. And the laundry basket.

Christmas Turkeys

Christmas might be a time of generosity for most people, but not for two silly security guards in the UK. Guarding a mobile-phone outlet in a shopping centre, the luckless pair seized their chance to enter the big time by stealing £1,500 worth of phones from the stockroom after the store alarm went off. Although they pinned the missing stock on a burglary carried out by someone they hadn't been quick enough to catch, CCTV footage revealed the truth and led to their swift arrest. The funny thing was, this all happened on Christmas Day, when the shopping centre wasn't even open, and all law-abiding citizens were at home eating turkey.

Thanks, Man

Not all criminals end up shame-faced after their arrest. In fact, a man from Florida actually thanked the cops who captured him, as they managed to reunite him with a bong he thought he'd lost, like, ages ago. After pulling the hopeless hippy over for having a faulty light, the police officers searched the boot of his car and quickly discovered the misplaced instrument. The delighted dude's elation was soon quashed when he was promptly charged with 'possession of a controlled substance' and 'intent to use'. Presumably he lost the bong for real that time.

FAIL

'I think that gay marriage should be between a man and a woman.'

Arnold Schwarzenegger

Drunken Dad

A Tennessee man got so drunk one Sunday afternoon he asked a ten-year-old to drive him home. After reaching speeds of over 90 mph, Junior Sterling Moss crashed the Ford Windstar van, hospitalizing all five of the vehicle's passengers, which included three children. The two adult passengers were found to have taken cocaine on top of the alcohol consumed, and, worse still, one of them was wearing a T-shirt bearing the legend 'Buy This Dad a Beer'.

Pin Head

Don't take betting tips from ex-taxi driver Trevor Agnew, unless you want to lose your stake, that is. The rather naïve cabbie from the UK stole several bank cards and tried to use them to withdraw cash, even though he didn't have access to the pin numbers. Agnew was filmed by police on a CCTV camera trying to gain access to the bank accounts by using random pin numbers at the same cashpoint, day after day. Given that the odds of a correct guess were about 1 in 10,000, the silly fool failed to withdraw a single penny. His only prize: three years in the slammer.

FAIL

'I am not worried about the deficit.
It is big enough to take care of itself.'

Ronald Reagan, fully in control

Own Goal

Andrew Kellett was branded 'Britain's Dumbest Criminal' after posting not one, not two, but eighty videos of himself engaged in illegal activity on YouTube. Clips included Kellett driving at 140 mph (which helpfully featured a shot of the speedometer), driving away from a petrol station without paying, and taking class-A drugs. City magistrates quickly dispensed justice, with one councillor noting, 'He has handed us the evidence against him on a plate. If more criminals were as obliging, the city would be even safer.'

FAIL

'I'm not Superman. I can't handle all of these women.'

Tommy Lee of Mötley Crüe

Birthday Boaster

A reckless Australian teen celebrated his seventeenth birthday in some style by crashing a car into a fence. The only problem was, he'd been disqualified from driving just three months previously and the car wasn't registered or insured. After fleeing the scene, the tearaway teen posted a (no doubt regretful) Facebook status that boasted of him losing control of a car at high speed and leaving the scene of a crash . . . which led police straight to his door.

Diamond Geezer

A jewellery thief in Spain gave himself away in delightful fashion when it was discovered he'd swallowed a diamond from a pendant that had been stolen just hours earlier. Stopped at a routine police checkpoint, the diamond muncher's vehicle was searched and the pendant was found . . . but the diamond was missing. Police grew suspicious when they noticed the man kept 'putting his hand to his mouth', so they swiftly whisked him to a medical centre, where X-rays revealed the prized stone sitting in his stomach. There was a 'little wait' before it could be returned to its rightful owner.

FAIL

'I even accept for the sake of argument that sexual orgies eliminate social tensions and ought to be encouraged.'

US Supreme Court justice Antonin Scalia, speaking to young people at Harvard University

PRINCE PHILIP, DUKE OF EDINBURGH:
Prince of Faux Pas

'You look like you're ready for bed.'

To the President of Nigeria, who was dressed in his national costume

'Do you work in a strip club?'

In conversation with a female sea cadet in 2010

'How do you keep the natives off the booze long enough to pass the test?'

To a Scottish driving instructor in 1995

'I thought it was against the law for a woman to solicit.'

On being introduced to a female solicitor in 1987

'No wonder you're deaf.'

To the children at a school for the deaf, during a performance by a steel band

'You can't have been here long: you haven't got a pot belly.'

To a tourist he met in Budapest

Bum Deal

Most people bring back a T-shirt as a souvenir of their holiday, apart from potty Englishman Nigel Ely, who was arrested by police after he stole Saddam Hussein's bronze buttocks from the statue of the fallen leader during a trip to Iraq. Defined as 'Iraqi cultural property', Saddam's arse saw Mr Ely taken into custody. He was not allowed to keep the bum.

Strictly Come Stealing

A pitiful criminal brought unwitting attention to his crime when he decided to dance while shoplifting in the clothing section of a K-Mart store. Presumably overcome by the shop's music, the light-footed man was captured on CCTV combining his two favourite pastimes: dancing and stealing. The resulting footage became a viral Internet sensation, accumulating over 100,000 hits in less than a week. But, thanks to his popularity, the 'Dancing Shoplifter' was quickly recognized and arrested.

FAIL
**'The streets are safe in Philadelphia.
It's only the people who make them unsafe.'**

Frank Rizzo, former mayor of Philadelphia

Tatt's a Fact

You'd think 'destroy the evidence' would be somewhere near the top of the to-do list for most criminals. Not so for Anthony Garcia, a member of the Rivera gang in Los Angeles who immortalized his involvement in the murder of a rival gang member by getting a tattoo of the crime scene inked on his chest. LA police had been struggling to solve the case for four years, but in 2008 Garcia was picked out from a mug shot in which the tattoo was clearly visible. After arresting Garcia, police officers posed as gang members in his cell, and the hapless hoodlum soon opened up about his involvement in the crime. The fact that he'd inked 'Rivera Kills' above the image of the crime scene can't have helped his case . . .

POWER FAIL

Ludicrous Leaders

It takes unwavering self-belief, unshakable confidence and clear vision to lead, and, judging by the following entries, mindless stupidity doesn't go amiss either. From the politicians who lead us into wars, to exquisitely bred members of the Royal Family, it appears that even the men we're supposed to respect are prone to the odd gaffe.

GEORGE W. BUSH:
Educationalizing the World

'I understand the importance of bondage between parent and child.'

Steady on, George

'More and more of our imports are coming from overseas.'

Just in case you didn't understand the nitty-gritty of trade

'It is white.'

When asked to describe the White House

'Do you have blacks too?'

To the president of Brazil

 'Solutions are not the answer.'

Richard Nixon, former US president

Silly Sausage

Appropriately named US politician Anthony Weiner resigned after 'sexting' a saucy picture of himself to a female follower on Twitter. After several days of denials, Weiner finally relented and resigned after shock jocks Opie & Anthony leaked the explicit photo of his, er, wiener.

Off Guard

A Buckingham Palace guard was asked to step down from his duties as a regimental guard for the wedding of Prince William and Catherine Middleton after he posted on his Facebook profile that sweet, smiley, heart-stealing Kate was a 'posh bitch'. Listing his interests as 'super-strength lager' and 'causing trouble', the rather misguided eighteen-year-old also found himself slapped with a Ministry of Defence investigation.

FAIL

'Politics gives guys so much power that they tend to behave badly around women. And I hope I never get into that.'

Bill Clinton

Sleeping on the Job

While we might sometimes find ourselves nodding off at work, at least we have the courtesy to do it at our desks. Not so the Swedish lay judge who, when presiding over a case of tax fraud in January 2012, decided to take a sneaky kip while court was in session. Despite being asleep while the evidence was being given, the judge decided to acquit the defendant – presumably because he was keen to get home and put his feet up.

FORMER US VICE-PRESIDENT DAN QUAYLE:
He Knows Where It's At

'It's a question of whether we're going to go forward into the future or past to the back.'

Hammering the message home

'It is wonderful to be here in the great state of Chicago.'

Master of geography

'I love California. I practically grew up in Phoenix.'

Not to break with tradition

'I was recently on a tour of Latin America, and the only regret I have was that I didn't study Latin harder in school so I could converse with those people.'

Linguistic titan

RONALD REAGAN:
Bright Spark

'I've noticed that everyone who is for abortion has already been born.'

Exercising his powers of logic

'I have left orders to be awakened at any time in case of national emergency, even if I'm in a cabinet meeting.'

Sleeping on the job

'What does an actor know about politics?'

Fortieth president of the United States and former actor

Happy Clamper

Hell hath no fury like a man with a clamp. Not least Gareth Andrews, a rather enthusiastic clamper who decided to place two of his immovable yellow brackets on royal-protection police cars in Portsmouth when Queen Elizabeth came for a visit. Having refused to remove the clamps, Andrews was later described in court as 'belligerent', 'defiant' and 'obstructive'. 'Pretty stupid' comes to mind too . . .

FAIL

**'Television won't matter in your
lifetime or mine.'**

Rex Lambert, the then editor of
the *Radio Times*, in 1936

Captain Not-So-Sensible

Traditionally pilots are figures of glamour, but the captain of Delta Flight 6132 let the side down when he got himself stuck in the toilet mid-flight between North Carolina and New York. Although he was found safe and well by a passenger, the situation very nearly caused an international incident when the equally silly co-pilot, who didn't understand the passenger's 'thick foreign accent', alerted air traffic control, thinking he was a terrorist.

FAIL

'Outside of the killings, Washington has one of the lowest crime rates in the country.'

Marion Barry, former mayor of Washington, DC

HEALTH FAIL

Flatlining Fools

When it comes to the world of health and medicine, men's dangly bits take centre stage. From truck drivers impaling themselves on compressed air hoses to men who, having got all excited in their pants, are unable to ever get unexcited – welcome to a man-fail minefield.

Numbskull

New Year's Eve is traditionally a night for over-indulging, but rarely do you get so drunk that you don't even realize you've been shot. In 2010 a Polish chap living in Germany went to his doctors after suffering persistent pains from a lump in his head. Following an X-ray, medics quickly discovered the lump was in fact a bullet that had long been lodged in the man's head. The forgetful man had a vague recollection of receiving a bump to his bonce while out celebrating New Year five years previously, but he'd been too drunk at the time to do anything about it.

FAIL

'A low voter turnout is an indication of fewer people going to the polls.'

Dan Quayle stating the obvious

Is That a Banana in Your Pocket?

A man in Iran was left with a permanent erection after having *'Borow be salaamat'* ('Good luck with your journeys') tattooed on his penis. The foolhardy chap was in considerable pain for a week afterwards before he realized 'it' was not going to go away. Iranian doctors reportedly advised that 'Based on our unique case, we discourage penile tattooing.'

FAIL

'We are ready for an unforeseen event that may or may not occur.'

Al Gore, former US vice-president

Put a Plug in It!

A New Zealand truck driver was taken to hospital after he 'blew up like a balloon' after 'slipping and falling' onto an air hose that pumped compressed air directly into his bottom. 'I was blowing up like a football,' he said. 'I felt the air rush into my body and I felt like it was going to explode.' After hearing the poor man's screams, his workmates managed to find the safety valve and turn it off, with doctors reporting later that 'He's lucky to be alive.' You mustn't laugh, though – it was very serious and not funny at all . . .

Sticky Situation

Superglue is the prankster's weapon of choice, as one poor Australian gentleman discovered to his cost when he found himself stuck to a toilet seat in a shopping-centre lavatory, the victim of a practical joke. Unfortunately medical staff were unable to extract the sorry soul from the seat onsite and were instead forced to prise the seat from the pan and carry the man through the mall, a king atop his throne. 'Industrial solvents' were eventually used to free him.

Burger Me!

Morgan Spurlock isn't the only one to have binged on McDonald's in the pursuit of fame. Take Don Gorske from Wisconsin, who in 2011 celebrated eating his 25,000th Big Mac. After thirty-nine years on his desultory diet, Guinness say Gorske holds the world record for the most Big Macs consumed by anyone, ever. Strangely, news reports didn't confirm how much the fifty-nine-year-old Gorske weighs.

FAIL

'I do not like this word "bomb". It is not a bomb. It is a device that is exploding.'

French ambassador to New Zealand and
Aotearoa Jacques le Blanc, in 1995

A Quick Sit-Down

While all of us might sometimes feel a little lonely, don't do as Le Xing of Hong Kong did and try and befriend an inanimate object. In 2008 emergency services were forced to extract Xing from a park bench after he'd wedged his penis into a metal pipe. Feeling in need of a friend – not to mention a little over-amorous – the rather misguided chap decided to make love to the wooden seat. Having failed to drain Xing of blood in an effort to deflate his penis, the emergency services were forced to cut away part of the bench and escort it and Xing to hospital, where it took doctors four hours to cut him free.

FAIL

> *'I'd love a drug that was good for you. I was*
> *thinking about Ecstasy with Vitamin B.'*
>
> Gavin Rossdale of Bush

Pead Off

Being rushed to hospital with a collapsed lung and suspected cancer is no laughing matter . . . unless doctors discover it's not cancer after all, but a pea plant growing inside you. This really did happen to a man in Massachusetts in 2010, who went to hospital after suffering difficulty breathing. Upon arrival, medical staff quickly discovered the root cause, telling the man that the pea must have 'gone down the wrong way', whereupon it sprouted. Worse, one of the first meals the man had in hospital after his surgery included – you guessed it – peas.

Petty Practice

Although it's good practice to keep an eye on your outgoings, try to keep the petty paybacks to a minimum. When Jason West of Salt Lake City's quibble over a $25 medical bill went unheeded, he decided to settle the remaining payment entirely in cents – all 2,500 of them. West's medical clinic failed to see the funny side, and he was charged with disorderly conduct.

FAIL

'I was a pilot flying an airplane and it just so happened that where I was flying made what I was doing spying.'

Francis Gary Power, US reconnaissance pilot, accused by the Soviet Union of spying

ImPATIENT

Why make a 999 call and wait an agonizing three minutes for the ambulance to arrive when you can just steal one that's parked nearby? Or so thought Floridian Hubert Lee Credit, who stole an ambulance to drive himself to hospital after he'd been beaten up. He only managed to get a mile away before the authorities pulled him over and whacked him in the slammer.

Ouch!

Just because it's possible to poke one thing into another thing doesn't mean you should go ahead and do it . . . as an Englishman learned to his cost when he got his penis stuck in a steel pipe. Rocking up to casualty with the pipe still firmly 'attached' to his member, the luckless chap was forced to surrender to the seven firefighters who'd been quickly enlisted to help with its removal. Which was done with a metal grinder.

CELEBRITY FAIL

Silly Stars

With all that media training, you would think the powerful men of the entertainment world would be able to stop themselves from uttering ridiculous things. Sadly, you would be wrong. Get thee to a media training class, celebrity men! Especially you, Charlie Sheen.

'The only time I use women in films
is when they're naked or dead.'

Thoroughly progressive film producer Joel Silver

Bale Out

Christian Bale has been nominated for countless
awards, including an Oscar and a BAFTA, and can
be commended for his involved 'method' preparation
for his acting roles. But since 2008 he will for ever be
known as 'that guy who went schizo at work', after
blowing his top on the set of *Terminator Salvation* at
the director of photography, who had the temerity to
move a light in his field of vision.

Mindless

Russell Crowe broke cinemagoers' hearts when he played troubled code-breaker and Nobel Prize-winning mathematical genius John Forbes Nash, Jr, in *A Beautiful Mind*. The film won countless awards and Russell himself won a BAFTA for Best Actor in 2002. But when part of his acceptance speech was cut from the television broadcast, he kicked off. After learning that his reading of the poem 'Sanctity' by Patrick Kavanagh had been cut, Crowe allegedly 'roughed up' television producer Malcolm Gerrie by pinning him against a wall and calling him a 'c**t'. He was later forced to publicly apologize, with some entertainment journalists suggesting the incident cost him an Oscar.

FAIL

'I have a couple of guys to do my laundry.
Just because I am lazy and rich.'

Kid Rock

Trump Card

Business magnate extraordinaire Donald Trump regularly tops the world's rich lists and is, naturally, the overlord of the US version of *The Apprentice*. As if that isn't already enough, he has also built or owns over a dozen skyscrapers and hotel resorts and he is married to a total fox called Melania. *But* he doesn't quite have everything: let us not forget he is also the owner of the most ridiculous bouffant comb-over known to man. How does he ever manage to convince anyone of anything in those top-level board meetings?

FAIL

'I don't feel we did wrong in taking this great country away from them. There were great numbers of people who needed new land, and the Indians were selfishly trying to keep it for themselves.'

John Wayne

Switched On

He might be able to run and kick balls with a finesse not seen since England's triumphant win at the World Cup in 1966, but Paul 'Gazza' Gascoigne's troubled relationship with booze saw him helping out his fishing pal, killer Raoul Moat in 2010. Talking to reporters after the fugitive Moat had shot a policeman, Gazza told a DJ on Metro Radio that he was off to talk to him. According to Gazza, everything was going to be OK because he had brought 'a can of lager, some chicken, a mobile phone and something to keep [Moat] warm'. Gazza later claimed he had not known about the shooting (which was just as well).

> **FAIL**
>
> *'I'll always remember 1995 as the year
> I found out Star Trek wasn't real.'*
>
> Daniel Johns, guitarist and lead singer of Silverchair

What a Jesse

Marriage to one of Hollywood's sweethearts wasn't enough for tattooed tearaway and motorcycle enthusiast Jesse James when he decided to cheat on his third wife, Sandra Bullock, with a collection of women. In March 2010 several of James's former conquests came forward to reveal details of their affairs with the married celebrity and Bullock promptly filed for divorce. Clearly a fan of nuptials, James has since had an on/off engagement to *LA Ink* star Kat Von D. Reports are unclear as to whether it's currently on or off.

Not Such a Winner

Hollywood A-lister Charlie Sheen has been no stranger to the headlines, but he underwent the mother of all meltdowns when, while on an extended break from the set of *Two and a Half Men* at the beginning of 2011, he set up home with a porn star and a model (collectively nicknamed the 'goddesses'). Locked in a spiral of drink and drug abuse, Sheen gave a series of interviews that showcased his increasingly erratic state. Despite repeated reassurance that he was 'winning', it was clear for all to see that Sheen wasn't in the rudest of health. Credit to the man, however – he made a valiant comeback to our screens in summer 2012, so let's watch this space.

CHARLIE SHEEN:
He's Got the Blood of a Tiger

'I'm different. I have a different constitution; I have a different brain; I have a different heart. I got tiger blood, man.'

Don't mess with him, people

'What does that mean? What's the cure? Medicine? Make me like them? Not gonna happen. I'm bi-winning. I win here. I win there.'

On being asked if he was bi-polar

'The nights I don't sleep it's because there's a higher calling telling me to stand guard.'

Ever heard of a God complex, Charlie Sheen?

'The run I was on made Sinatra, Flynn, Jagger, Richards, all of them just look like droopy-eyed, armless children.'

Partying harder than Keith Richards is some boast

'It's perfect. It's awesome. Every day is just filled with just wins. All we do is put wins in the record books. We win so radically in our underwear before our first cup of coffee, it's scary.'

Who needs clothes when you can win in your boxer shorts!

FAIL

> *'There are, I think, three countries left in the world where I can go and I'm not as well known as I am here. I'm a pretty big star, folks – I don't have to tell you. Superstar, I guess you could say.'*
>
> Bruce Willis

Bunga Bunga!

A politician and media tycoon who has thrice served as Italy's prime minister, Silvio Berlusconi is a powerful man. Yet the thing he'll be remembered for is his penchant for women. Lots and lots of them. Worse still, after leaving office in 2011, Berlusconi released an album of love songs. Michael Bublé he ain't.

Silly Bob Thornton

Billy Bob Thornton has appeared in over seventy films, has walked on the arm of Hollywood siren Angelina Jolie and has won an Oscar. He's also in a band called the Boxmasters. But if you interview him and his band, you're not allowed to mention his pre-music fame; or the acting; or the Oscar; or the seventy films; or wearing a vial of Angelina's blood round his neck – because none of that has absolutely anything to do with how you might have heard of his amazing band. As the Canadian Broadcasting Corporation found out to its cost, when Thornton had a huge strop live on the radio, refusing to talk to host Jian Ghomeshi. As the (very polite) veteran DJ said afterwards, 'To not answer questions because I made the apparently egregious mistake of calling him an actor as well as a musician, it just seemed a little absurd.'

*'There is certainly more in the future
now than back in 1964.'*

Roger Daltrey

TOM CRUISE:
Man Fail of the Scientology Kind

'You don't know the history of psychiatry. I do.'
To Matt Lauer of NBC's *Today Show* when he was supposed
to be on a publicity junket for *War of the Worlds*

**'Talk is over-rated as a means of settling
disputes.'**
Use your fists instead?

**'When you talk about emotional, chemical
imbalances in people, there is no science
behind that.'**
So says Dr Cruise

FAIL

**'If we're not supposed to eat animals,
how come they're made out of meat?'**
Tom Snyder, host of NBC's *Tomorrow Show*

FAIL

*'You need to respect me.
You are taking away my shine!'*

Bobby Brown, to fellow pop star Usher
at Usher's – *not Bobby's* – birthday party

A Prince Among Men

Ah, Prince Philip, husband of Elizabeth I, the Queen of England, how we adore your inability to be diplomatic when in earshot of anyone 'foreign'. There are quite a few gaffes to count, so let's just pick one at random. Like the time he visited a project tasked with protecting endangered turtle doves in Anguilla in 1965. He was reported to have quipped, 'Cats kill far more birds than men. Why don't you have a slogan: "Kill a cat and save a bird"?'

> FAIL
>
> *'In an action film you act in the action;*
> *in a drama film you act in the drama.'*
>
> Jean-Claude Van Damme

Not Out of the Woods Yet . . .

International golf whizz and all-round family man Tiger Woods lost a great deal of his sizable income – not to mention his dignity – when he was caught out having not one, not two but multiple affairs behind his beautiful wife's back. Tiger's troubles came to light when he crashed his car into a fire hydrant, a tree and several hedges after an argument with his beloved. Reports revealed she'd attacked Tiger's car with a golf club, and allegedly his face with her fists, after she found out about the first affair. Proving he's not fussy when it comes to the fairer sex, Tiger was revealed to have shacked up with a variety of ladies, from porn stars to a waitress in his local diner. Despite the pro-golfer's remorse, he and his wife divorced in 2010 . . . and no one can quite look at him in the same way again.

FAIL

'I don't own a gun. I own about 150 guns.'

Lead singer of Metallica and firearm
enthusiast James Hetfield

FAIL

*'I'm one of those people you hate
because of genetics.'*

Brad Pitt

Starry-Eyed

Ever since John Lennon acknowledged that Ringo
Starr might not have been the best drummer in
the world ('He's not even the best drummer in the
Beatles!'), many theories about his lack of rhythm
have been posited. One even argues that his below-
par timekeeping made for a style of syncopated
drumming that was quite literally hypnotic. In any
event, Ringo has had quite enough of your talk and
messing, which was why he posted an online video
in 2008 telling the world he was never going to send
out another autograph for as long as he lived. 'PEACE
AND LOVE!' he bellowed. 'I'M WARNING YOU
WITH PEACE AND LOVE. NO MORE FAN MAIL.'

FAIL

'A bachelor's life is no life for a single man.'

Samuel Goldwyn

FAIL

'Yo, I failed ninth grade three times, but I don't think it was necessarily 'cause I'm stupid.'

Eminem

FAIL

'If I did that, I'd be sticking my head in a moose.'

Samuel Goldwyn, film producer extraordinaire
and no stranger to malapropisms

DOMESTIC FAIL

Hapless Homemakers

A man doesn't feel more at home than when he's got a paintbrush in one hand and a can of beer in the other. But it's not always a smooth ride, for in this chapter we shall encounter man failure on a domestic level. From tales of DIY disasters, including one man who pinned himself to the wall with his own nail gun, to escapades in the garden, including one brave soul who hit the headlines for pruning his roses in the nude, it's all here as a lesson to us all. As the following true-life tales will prove, anything that can happen in the home can go horribly wrong in the home. So if you don't mind our saying so, men, it might be time to call in the professionals.

No More Nails

An American man learned just how dangerous a nail gun can be when he managed to fire a 3.5-inch nail into his skull. Catching up on a bit of DIY at home, the cack-handed chap didn't register the nail entering his head and only went to hospital the next day on the advice of his girlfriend after he complained about feeling nauseous. The X-ray showed the huge nail was embedded right in the centre of his brain. Let's hope it knocked some sense into him.

FAIL

'I think she'd rather have a nice, intimate wedding and, in a way, so would I. But the networks like me . . . I'm a ratings machine.'

Donald Trump on televizing his wedding
to Melania Knauss

'Who is the erection police?'

Rapper and thong-enthusiast Sisqo, after he found out that, according to Mississippi law, 'It is illegal for a male to be sexually aroused in public.'

Cocked Up

British teenager Rory McInnes's parents were no doubt initially quite pleased with themselves when they managed to enlist their son in a spot of DIY. They weren't so pleased, however, to receive a call from the press some time later to inform them that their son's efforts had amounted to a 60-ft penis painted on the flat roof of their home. McInnes's handiwork had gone unnoticed for a year, and by this point the crafty teen was away travelling on his gap year. When his parents called to quiz him about the painted cock, he simply quipped, 'Oh, you've found it, then.'

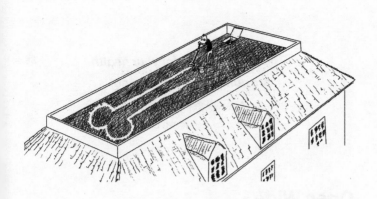

FAIL

'I have big nuts. Huge nuts. Elephantitis
of the balls – that's what I have.'

Eminem

FAIL

*'The best activities for your health
are pumping and humping.'*

Arnold Schwarzenegger

Open Wide . . .

While it's common to find teeth-fiddlers a little bit scary, few would attempt to turn the tables and scare the dentist by turning up for their check-up completely starkers, as one chap in Connecticut did. The receptionist screamed, the man ran away, and police arrested him for public indecency. To make matters even worse, the disorganized fool had been a whole five days late for his scheduled appointment.

Pie-Eyed

Tony Johnson from Lancashire had an original take on the idea of keeping mascots when he inexplicably decided to keep a burnt pie on top of his mantelpiece for nearly forty years. Mr Johnson told newspaper reporters that the pie, which had originally been over-baked in 1972, had become a talisman that he and his family would take with them on their travels to foreign climes. 'Wherever we go, the pie comes with us. It's been on holiday with us every year and it even has its own deckchair, fly hat and sombrero.' He also claimed it brought him luck, after he and the pie won nearly $7,000 during a holiday in Las Vegas.

> FAIL
>
> *'Girls are like pianos. When they're not upright, they're grand.'*
>
> Benny Hill

Beetle Bum

Perhaps there should be rules about doing DIY on your roof. Certainly when you're using bitumen, one of the stickier substances known to man, and definitely when you're over ninety years old. Just ask the elderly German man who managed to get stuck to his roof after he slipped and fell on the black, tar-like coating. Finding himself stuck with nowhere to go, the poor soul was later described by police as looking like 'a beetle on its back'. He was eventually unstuck by firefighters, and no doubt sworn never to climb atop his roof again.

FAIL

'My friends, no matter how rough the
road may be, we can and we will never,
never surrender to what is right.'

Dan Quayle

> **'Chemistry is a class you take in high school
> or college where you figure out two plus
> two is ten or something.'**
>
> Dennis Rodman, former NBA basketball player

DIY Disaster

One enthusiastic homemaker accidentally got a lump of gloss paint right in his eye while he indulged in a spot of painting and decorating. It splashed straight onto his eyelash, and although he tried to ignore it, it began to stick his eyes together. In a complete panic, the rather foolhardy chap tried to wipe away the offending gloss with white spirit. Rather unsurprisingly the kindly folk at A&E advised him that white spirit is far worse than paint.

Put the Nail Gun Down!

A warning to all would-be DIY-ers: stick to using adhesives that don't have the potential to penetrate skin (and bone). Or, at the very least, read up on the potential hazards before attempting to use anything that comes with a safety warning. Unfortunately one (of many, it seems) poor chap learned the hard way when he decided to use a nail gun to attach a home-made wooden storage box to a wall in his kitchen. The inevitable ensued when the silly sausage decided to fire his gun while the two bits of wood he was nailing together were still in his hand. The nail gun went off and shot a 15-mm nail right through his fingertip. If that wasn't already painful enough, the man decided to save on answering any embarrassing questions that might be asked at the hospital by immediately removing the nail himself with a pair of pliers. Ouch!

Birthday Suit

Enthusiastic naturist Kevin Lavelle took a shine to tackling his household chores in the nude – much to the chagrin of his neighbours. The court heard how Lavelle would wash his car, clear out the guttering and change the wheels on his car with everything on show. 'He would stand against a wall with nothing on,' said a neighbour. 'He caused real upset.'

Melting Moment

When a man in the US tried to melt ice on his porch with a blowtorch, he managed to set fire not only to his own apartment, but also to the flats two floors above it. Local fire chiefs said the chap's mistake had been to hook the blowtorch up to a 20-pound propane cylinder, which resulted in 25 firemen being called in to put the blaze out. Perhaps next time he should try using a hairdryer.

An Explosive Read

A man in Florida flexed his interior-design muscles a little too far when he used a live WWII hand-grenade as a bookend. After leaving the grenade alone for sixty years while it sat on the shelf propping up his encyclopedias, the chap decided quite inexplicably to take the pin out. Immediately regretting his actions, he put the pin back in. And then he threw the grenade to the bottom of the garden, where a bomb-disposal team was forced to perform a controlled detonation.

Ready, Aim, Fire!

Poor old Nigel Kirk from Staffordshire forgot to obey the first rule of nail-gunning: remove all obstacles from the floor before taking your first shot. In the middle of a tricky floor-boarding job, Kirk slipped on a towel and fired a 5-cm nail straight into his heart. Astonishingly, the cack-handed fool didn't even realize what he'd done until he tried to take off his jumper, but failed because the nail was pinning it to his chest. One ambulance and a three-hour operation to remove the nail later, and medical staff told reporters he'd missed an artery by just millimetres.

First Class

Puerile postman David Goodman employed an unusual tactic to help brighten the day of one poor unsuspecting woman on his rounds. Having noticed that a female employee of a law firm in Wisconsin 'seemed to be stressed out', he decided to 'cheer her up' by removing his clothes to deliver her mail. Unsurprisingly, she wasn't impressed as the misguided mailman was arrested for 'lewd and lascivious behaviour'.

Barefoot Dave

Englishman Dave Richards tried to ease the pain of the weekly food shop by buying his groceries *sans* shoes. However, his local supermarket chain didn't take so kindly, banning him on the grounds of 'health and safety'. Richards claimed he'd stopped wearing shoes completely after a physiotherapist had told him it would cure his limp. Said Richards, 'I particularly enjoy wearing a dinner suit and being barefoot, which I think is very classy.' He did, however, confess that his wife found the whole no-shoes thing rather embarrassing, admitting, 'We have an arrangement where I don't go to particular places with her.'

Bullseye!

The amateur gardener has many useful tools at his disposal – the humble spade, the reliable trowel. But accidents can still happen, like when Arizona resident Leroy Luetscher slipped and fell headfirst onto his secateurs, impaling himself through the eye and forcing the blades deep into his skull. Incredibly, doctors were not only able to remove the implement, but also to rebuild Luetscher's eye socket, leaving him with merely a 'slight swelling in his eyelids and minor double vision.'

FAIL

'If you've seen one redwood tree, you've seen them all.'

Ronald Reagan

Hold the Line, Please

Common sense and etiquette would suggest that it's unwise to talk on your mobile phone while you're having a tinkle. But a man in China failed to heed this advice when, in October 2010, he tried to retrieve his phone after dropping it into the toilet. But the phone proved elusive and the poor chap ended up shoulder-deep in pipework, not to mention very stuck. It took ten unfortunate minutes to release the sorry soul from his shackles – all ten minutes of which were broadcast on state television.

> FAIL
>
> *'I haven't committed a crime.*
> *What I did was fail to comply*
> *with the law.'*
>
> Ronald Reagan

The Second Coming

Leaving bacon frying unattended is of course very silly, but for Englishman Toby Elles it proved something of a divine revelation. In March 2010 he fell asleep while cooking some rashers and woke up sometime later when the pan started to smoke. Not only had Elles managed to save his house from certain fire, he was also delighted to discover that a spookily detailed image of Jesus had etched itself onto the bottom of his frying pan. Showing off Jesus to the press, Elles said, 'I'm going to keep it for the rest of my life.' No, Toby Elles, put it in the bloody dishwasher!

I'll Have a Burger With . . . Zzzzzz

When a man with a serious case of the munchies in Tennessee discovered there was nothing to eat in his house, he didn't let being drunk or tired stop him from taking a quick trip to McDonald's. Police reports later revealed the man was found asleep in the drive-thru lane at 6 a.m., apparently having nodded off as soon as staff had taken his burger order. He was arrested before he could eat anything.

FAIL

'See, in my line of work you've got to keep repeating things over and over again for the truth to sink in, to kind of catapult the proaganda.'

George W. Bush

FAIL

'For NASA, space is still a high priority.'

Dan Quayle

Bricking It

It's perhaps unwise to tackle a skilled trade if you have no previous experience. Just ask the daft senior citizen in Germany whose misguided attempt at bricklaying resulted in him imprisoning himself in his own cellar. After several days of internment, he eventually freed himself by destroying not only his own handiwork, but also that of his neighbour, by bashing down an adjoining wall. The neighbour wasn't amused, and the would-be DIY-er was charged with trespassing when he finally emerged from the wreckage.

'I wish they had wiener farms, 'cause then maybe I could get a bigger one.'

Mark Hoppus, bassist and lead vocalist from Blink 182

Happy Christmas, Man

While it's commendable to think of the environment at Christmas time, perhaps it's not so wise to decorate a large cannabis plant instead of the usual spruce. However, Englishman Ian Richards threw caution to the wind and adorned a jazz tobacco plant with baubles and tinsel in 2011. You can imagine him sitting in its pretty glow – at least until the police found it (and the rest of his home-grown), whereupon he was forced to spend the rest of the festivities behind bars.

Grow Up

A twenty-nine-year-old man in Georgia with a rather retrograde attitude to housework pulled a gun on his own mother when she refused to do his ironing. Police were called to the house after his poor old mum managed to escape following six hours' imprisonment. Her son had also confiscated her house keys and mobile phone, telling police he'd done it because ironing was 'woman's work'.

One Man in a Boat

A fifty-year-old man in England went to fairly extreme lengths to escape his wife when he took his homemade, half-finished boat out to sea for a bit of breathing space. After going missing for two days, the thoroughly fed-up chap eventually drifted into the path of a passing yacht, whereupon a lifeboat rescued him. 'It had no windows, just holes,' said the coastguard, referring to the makeshift vessel.

Heads Up!

When you buy your first home, money is invariably a little tight, but perhaps it's wise to spend spare cash on hiring a professional decorator. In keeping with this thrifty theme, one chap decided not only to tackle painting the walls of his new house himself, he also thought he'd make use of an old pot of paint he found in his mum's shed. To loosen the paint mixture he stirred it with a piece of wire secured to the end of an electric drill. The makeshift whisk seemed to work its magic because, after a good bit of stirring, the paint looked to be good as new. Climbing up the ladder, paint pot and brush in hand, his proud wife beaming up at him, the domestic titan began to tackle the job in hand . . . until, that is, the bottom of the paint tin fell out. It seems that while the wire had mixed the paint, it had also perforated the bottom of the paint can, causing gallons of white emulsion to pour all over the man's wife, the walls and the floor. Imagine how much that cost to clean up!

FAIL

*'I pick my nose and I'm not ashamed to admit it.
If there's a bogey, then just pick it, man.'*

Justin Timberlake

Otherwise Engaged

John Long of Somerset made good use of his retirement when he decided to turn a disused red phonebox into a toilet. Speaking to news outlets in 2010, the seventy-three-year-old pensioner said he had 'done lots of projects, but this is one of the biggest'. Proud of his phonebox-cum-privy, Long said, 'It's worked out extremely well.'

FAIL

*'The doctors X-rayed my head
and found nothing.'*

Jay Hanna 'Dizzy' Dean, Major League baseballer

'My only regret in the theatre is that I could never sit out front and watch me.'

Actor John Barrymore didn't mince his words

What a Turkey

Cooking Christmas dinner is a huge endeavour, but if you're having trouble with your timings, perhaps you should call your mum before turning to the emergency services. Sadly this didn't occur to one chap, who rang the police to ask, 'How long do you defrost a turkey for?' The operator then asked if, bar the Turkey Problem, there's 'a genuine emergency', to which the nitwit replied, 'It is an emergency. Do I take the giblets out before I defrost it?'

Don't Forget Your Keys

Police were called to a flat in Colchester, England after a member of the public reported witnessing a break-in at the property. Arriving on the scene and armed with tasers, police observed the supposed burglar attacking a boarded-up window with a sledgehammer, seemingly unbothered by the racket he was making. The only problem? He was breaking into his own house after locking himself out. Red faces all round, then.

SPORT AND HOBBY
FAIL

Downtime Dolts

It's tiring being a man, so they can be forgiven for wanting to kick back and relax. However, as the following tales of loony lorry drivers and football fanatics reveal, a man with too much time on his hands is a very dangerous thing.

FAIL *'Pitching is 80 per cent of the game.
The other half is hitting and fielding.'*

Baseball player Mickey Rivers

What's in a Name?

Proving that baby names should always be pre-agreed is Danny Pierce, an Everton Football Club supporter and father of an unfortunately named child. Calling his third daughter 'Eva-Toni-Ann' (see what he did there?) after his wife agreed they could pull the baby's name 'out of a hat', Pierce confessed, 'I'm Everton berserk. I always said if I had a daughter, she'd be called Eva-Toni-Ann . . . Even Liverpool fans think it's great.' Eva's mother, however, was not so enthusiastic: 'I'm not interested in football,' she told reporters.

And the Winner Is . . .

A seemingly lucky man in Salt Lake City was the envy of his town when he won a Lamborghini worth $200,000 in a contest at a convenience store. Although he was filmed jumping up and down with delight after his win, the poor chap's happiness didn't last long. He faced a battle to keep up with the six-monthly insurance payments – a staggering $2,400 apiece, plus taxes. But perhaps the biggest fly in the ointment was that he managed to crash the car just six hours after his win. 'I'm going to sell it,' he conceded, wisely, as the car sat in the garage being (very expensively) repaired.

Ice With That?

A twenty-three-year-old man from Queensland, Australia, was arrested for drink-driving a motorized cool box that he'd bought from eBay. Three times over the legal limit, the silly fool was also unable to produce a licence for his 'vehicle' and was promptly charged.

Unputdownable

A bus driver in the UK found himself the unwitting star of YouTube when he was secretly filmed by a passenger steering the bus with his elbows while reading a book. The soon-to-be Internet sensation was posted on the video-sharing website and swiftly prompted an investigation by the bus operator. Presumably his excuse was, it was just a really, really good book, but it's doubtful 'So good, you'll drive while reading it' was printed on the cover.

FAIL

'You guys pair up in groups of three, then line up in a circle.'

Bill Peterson, one-time American-football coach

Get a Lorry Load of That

A Romanian lorry driver sprang to fame when he decided to film himself doing an impromptu dance routine to break up his boring motorway journey. The truck driver can be seen in the footage waving his arms around, taking off his seatbelt and getting out of his seat, all the while driving perilously close to other vehicles. Sadly he was also silly enough to send the footage to a TV station, though news reports are unclear as to whether or not he was eventually captured. So keep your eyes peeled for a dancing lorry driver and, er, keep your distance.

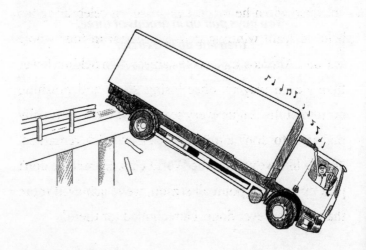

FAIL

**'Women should be all dressed in white,
like all other domestic appliances.'**

Bernie Ecclestone, Formula One racing chief, at the Indy 500,
after Danica Patrick finished fourth (the highest ever placing
by a woman in the event)

Always Look on the Bright Side of Life

Under-fourteens Huncoat United football manager Paul Chadwick gave new meaning to the term 'eternal optimist' when he made a meal out of celebrating his beloved team winning their first point in four whole seasons. After losing seventy games, often fielding fewer than eleven players, once losing 25–0, and finishing bottom of the league every season, the team eventually managed to draw a mighty 3–3. Chadwick remarked, 'It feels like we've won the World Cup. Even if we don't pick up another point all season, we've achieved more than we have ever done. I am chuffed for them.'

> **'Half this game is 90 per cent mental.'**
>
> Danny Ozark, one-time Major League baseball manager

Customer Service

Grimsby Town Football Club, UK got the complaint letter to end them all when a disgruntled fan wrote a 700-word missive to his beloved team lamenting his treatment as a customer. Highlights included: 'I could take any of my 4,000 customers at random, burn down their houses, impregnate their wives and then dismember their children before systematically sending them back in the post, limb-by-limb, and still ensure a level of customer satisfaction which exceeds that which I have experienced at Blundell Park.' Naturally the letter spread like wildfire on the Internet, causing the club considerable embarrassment.

FAIL

'Sure there have been injuries and deaths in boxing, but none of them serious.'

Alan Minter, former British middleweight boxer

No. 1 Fan

An Englishman living in Australia travelled 10,000 miles and spent over £700 to see his football team, Blackburn Rovers, play – but still missed the match due to a broken-down train. Will Keegan flew by plane from Melbourne to London and then hoped to go on to Manchester by train. But an hour into the final leg, the train stopped due to torn-down power lines. Keegan eventually arrived in Manchester a whole eight hours after kick-off to discover his team had beaten the opposition 2–0. Forced to return to Australia just a couple of days later without having watched a single match, Keegan was reported to be 'devastated'.

FAIL

'Without censorship, things can get
terribly confused in the public mind.'
US Army General William Childs Westmoreland

'It's very important for folks to
understand that when there's more
trade, there's more commerce.'

George W. Bush

Interesting Hobby ...

In 2009 an engineer (with perhaps a little too much
time on his hands) won the world record for the 'longest
ever flight by a paper plane'. The fifty-two-year-old
president of the Japan Origami Airplane Association
managed to keep his plane airborne for 27.9 seconds,
telling the *Daily Telegraph* that his dream was to launch
a paper aircraft from space. Mind your heads!

FAIL

**'Congratulations on breaking my record.
I always thought it would stand until
it was broken.'**

Yogi Berra, Baseball Hall of Fame player and
manager, in a telegram to Johnny Bench,
world-beating catcher

'If only faces could talk...'

Pat Summerall, former American-football
player and television sportscaster

Eau de Locker Room

The makers of *Football Manager* found a novel way to
promote their video game when they decided to bottle
the 'smell of the locker room' and give it away as a free
gift. Apparently smelling of 'grass, sweat, boot leather
and heat spray', the aftershave was said by spokesman
Miles Jacobson to 'bring the dressing room into the
homes of *Football Manager 2009* players, inspiring
them for pre-match team talks, preparing them to
direct their team from the sidelines and prime them
for a tricky press conference'. Sounds yummy.

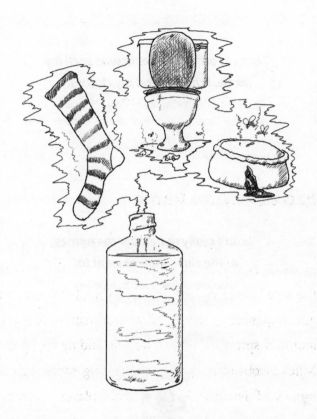

FAIL

'Nobody in football should be called a genius.
A genius is a guy like Norman Einstein.'

Former American-football quarterback and
NFL commentator Joe Theismann

'That's so when I forget how to spell my name, I can still find my clothes.'

Stu Grimson, Canadian ice-hockey player, who kept a photograph of himself above his locker

FAIL

'I can't really remember the names of the clubs that we went to.'

Shaquille O'Neal, asked by reporters whether he'd visited the Parthenon

Mouthful

Let's hope Londoner Charlie Bell has got himself a new hobby, because the old one was pretty disgusting. In May 2009 Bell appeared on Sky TV breaking the Guinness world record for 'the most maggots moved by the mouth in one hour'. Mr Bell's odd feat involved stuffing his mouth with over 15 kg of maggots and moving them from one container to another. Just why is anyone's guess.

FAIL

*'The similarities between me
and my father are different.'*

Dale Berra, former Major League baseball player

Lightweight

Fireman Alberto Arroyo landed himself in murky waters after posting online a video of himself competing in a bodybuilding competition while on sick leave. After suffering a back injury that strangely stopped him from fighting fires, but not from lifting heavy weights with well-oiled muscles in front of an admiring panel, Arroyo had been signed off permanently from his job. Following the discovery of his misdemeanour, he was fired after refusing to return to work.

FAIL

*'Strangely, in slow-motion replay, the ball
seemed to hang in the air for even longer.'*

David Acfield, former cricketer for Essex and an Olympic fencer

'Because I'm rich.'

Italian footballer Mario Balotelli, when
asked by police after crashing his car
why he had £5,000 in his back pocket

Jesus Lives

In 2008 Kirk Harper of Texas claimed to have seen the
image of Jesus on the wings of a moth. Harper told
reporters, 'I immediately thought it looked like Jesus
and that was what was so cool, 'cause you've seen his
face in grilled cheese sandwiches and windows and
things, but on a moth's back . . . we thought that was
pretty neat.'

FAIL

'Boxing's all about getting the job done as quickly as possible, whether it takes ten or fifteen or twenty rounds.'

Frank Bruno, former heavyweight boxer

FAIL

'I want all the kids to do what I do, to look up to me. I want all the kids to copulate me.'

Former Major League baseball player Andre Dawson, when asked how he felt about being a role model to children

BUSINESS FAIL

Idiots of Industry

In their working lives, it would appear that powerful men encounter a fair few problems – not least pesky things like 'tax' and 'justifying the enormous profits of one's mega-corporation'. So in this chapter we salute the thoroughly panicked behaviour of champions of industry, as they do their damnedest to keep their heads above water. From misjudged press releases and clumsily pulled sickies to baggage handlers who try on passengers' clothes and dotty inventions, it seems no business is immune to embarrassment.

An Education

During a careers talk to a group of eighth-grade students guest-speaker William Fried listed 'exotic dancing' and 'stripping' as alternative careers in a presentation called 'The Secret of a Happy Life'. Fried is reported to have told young women the bigger their bust size, the greater their earning potential as strippers. He also wrote in a handout, 'I majored in dating, drinking and gambling, and achieved superior marks in all of the categories.' It's not clear whether he was invited back the following year.

FAIL

'Sometimes they write what I say and not what I mean.'

Dominican Republic-born
Major League baseball player
Pedro Guerrero

> **'We're going to turn this team around 360 degrees.'**
>
> Jason Kidd, Dallas Mavericks
> basketball team

Please Leave a Massage

Competition is healthy for business, but not all businessmen can be trusted to play fair. In 2005 the founder of a New York company that provided a telephone answering service for doctors was charged with computer tampering after hacking into his competitor's services in an attempt to get ahead. Bemused patients calling to make appointments started to get either a busy signal or, in some cases, the sound of 'sexual moaning'. Some people pay a lot more money for those sorts of calls!

Do Not Disturb

Office parties are known for their high jinks, but a group of male hotel workers in Sweden took a drunken prank too far when they lodged a colleague behind a wall-mounted bed during a staff party. Trapped dangling by his head for over half an hour, the man was eventually rescued when the emergency services detached the bunk bed from the wall and took him straight to hospital with injuries to his throat and neck. It was reported the pranksters felt 'pretty bad' about their antics.

FAIL

'What do you think you're looking at, sugar t*ts?'

Mel Gibson, to his (female)
arresting officer in 2006

What a Twit

A foolhardy chap from Michigan lost his job as the
social media strategist for Chrysler when he slagged
off the driving skills of the motorcity on Twitter.
Thinking he was Tweeting from his personal account,
the twit typed, 'I find it ironic that Detroit is known

as the #motorcity and yet no one here knows how to f**king drive.' Although the man was promptly sacked by Chrysler, rival car manufacturers Ford inexplicably decided to hire him as their social media community manager, presumably after teaching him how to log in and out of his accounts properly.

No Touching

When local licensing laws make it difficult for you to run a club in which women dance with absolutely no clothes on, you might have to get creative. Which is exactly what the proprietor of the Erotic City strip club in Idaho decided to do when he ran an 'Art Night'. With punters given sketchpads and pencils to draw the (now G-string-less) girls, this slightly raunchy approach to the traditional night-school life-drawing class didn't fool local police officers, who visited the club and promptly charged the owner.

First Impressions Count

Keeping a personal blog when you work for arguably the most powerful company on the Internet isn't the wisest thing. Silly Mark Jen found out the hard way when he decided to start a new blog on the same day he began working for Google. After writing a post about his first day at the new company, he then thought it prudent to tell the blogosphere about Google's financial position. He was fired just eleven days later.

Sackie

A bank intern in the US pulled the ultimate sickie fail when he forgot to adjust his Facebook privacy settings after emailing his colleagues to tell them he couldn't come into work the next day. While his email claimed a 'family emergency' meant he'd have to leave town for a few days, his Facebook wall suggested differently – a recently posted photo of him grinning happily with a beer in one hand and a wand in the other implied the 'family emergency' was shorthand for 'wicked fancy-dress party = two-day hangover'. Unluckily for him, his bosses spotted the snap and sent a quick email informing him he was sacked, not without first attaching the incriminating photo, alongside the catty comment 'Cool wand.'

Ego Trip

A boon to lazy journalists and students cramming for exams, Wikipedia often gets a bad rap, and sometimes for good reason – beware those who edit entries to make themselves look better. Former MTV VJ and Internet entrepreneur Adam Curry took facts into his own hands when he edited the Wikipedia entry on podcasting. Curry allegedly removed reference to Kevin Marks (another Internet pioneer) so it looked liked Curry was the sole inventor of podcasting. He later explained, 'I edited out the Marks part . . . I realized I was in error.' Busted!

Fancy Dress

Australian airline Qantas was forced to install more CCTV cameras in baggage-handling areas after it was discovered one of its employees had been having fun with things that didn't belong to him. Delving into one suitcase, the baggage handler removed a camel costume, put it on and proceeded to drive around the tarmac on a baggage cart, in full view of passengers in the terminal. Spotted by the owner of the costume, the man was promptly sacked.

FAIL

'It's a vast waste of space.'

Prince Philip describing the British Embassy
in Berlin at its royal opening in 2000

What a Dummy

Not to be outdone, Austrian-born French tailor Franz Reichelt, or the 'Flying Tailor' as he became known, spent years designing a coat that pilots could wear to help save their fall should they have to leave their aircraft suddenly. Having successfully convinced the Parisian authorities to let him test his coat with a dummy from the first level of the Eiffel Tower, when the day came, in 1912, Reichelt changed his mind and decided to try the suit himself. Needless to say, his fancy coat failed him and he came to a grisly end underneath Paris's most famous landmark.

FAIL

'I've always thought that under-populated countries in Africa are vastly under-polluted.'

Chief economist of the World Bank Lawrence Summers,
on why toxic waste should be exported to Third World countries

A Wing and a Prayer

Henry Smolinski wanted to go one better than his namesake Henry Ford and make a car that flew. His invention, the AVE Mizar, was essentially a pimped-up 1971 Ford Pinto with flight controls, a Cessna engine and wings. Determined to pursue the idea of a road-worthy car that also doubled as a flight deck, the Mizar just about survived its test flight but did not fare so well when Smolinski tried it out for a second time. Both he and the other passenger were killed when the AVE Mizar's wings fell off.

Bird Brain

The first century's Ismail ibn Hammad al-Jawhari rather unwisely thought it'd be a good idea to use two homemade wooden wings to test man's ability to fly. The misguided nitwit is thought to have died when he jumped from the top of a mosque in an effort to test his invention. Prior to jumping, he was reported to have said, 'O people! No one has ever tried what I am about to do right now. I am going to fly now. The most important thing to do in this world is flying.' Poor Ismail.

FAIL

'Some women would prefer having smaller babies.'

Joseph Cullman, chairman of the tobacco company Philip Morris, when confronted with statistics that showed the effects of smoking during pregnancy

Silly Willies

Two men in Pittsburgh (somewhat wisely) failed to lodge their invention with the patent office when they devised the Whizzinator – a fake-penis device that allowed people to fraudulently pass alcohol and drug tests. 'The prosthetic penis is very realistic and concealing is simple,' they proudly claimed on their website. 'The Whizzinator will let it flow again and again, anytime, anywhere you need it!' Needless to say, the two men were charged with conspiracy in 2008.

FAIL

'Every time I reach a Starbucks, I feel like I've accomplished something, when actually I have accomplished nothing.'

A Houston man who set himself the (some might say entirely pointless) task of buying a coffee from every one of Starbucks' 6,000 outlets

Hacked Off

Before digital technology the best way to find out what was really happening at work was to keep close to the photocopier, just in case anything interesting was accidently left there. *LA Times* editorial and opinion editor Michael Kinsley learned this lesson the hard way after leaving details of a staff shake-up (which included one firing) on the photocopier, where it was promptly found by his staff. Another disaster soon followed when Kinsley's proposal to allow readers to rewrite *LA Times* articles online ended in tears when readers started adding swear words to published articles. Kinsey resigned just months later.

Bad Smell

Philip Mason from Newcastle, UK was prone to flatulence, but he took matters to the extreme when he seemed to take a little too much delight in asphyxiating his colleagues with his own brand of smell. After he'd failed to heed repeated warnings from above to stop pumping foul air into the office, Mason was fired. Co-workers were no doubt relieved that an end had been brought to the noxious honk, although one was heard to quip, 'At least when the head honchos from central office turned up, you could rely on Philip to get rid of them.'

WILDLIFE FAIL

Man v Beast

According to legend, St Francis of Assisi, the patron saint of animals, was so utterly in tune with nature he was able to persuade a wolf to put aside his bloodlust and stop eating people. He would, however, be horrified by the human brethren we're about to chronicle, especially the budgie smugglers (sadly not a euphemism in this case).

Something Fishy

While it's commendable to attempt to get busy in the kitchen, it's better to buy your ingredients for your tasty dinner rather than steal them. A greedy chap in Mississippi flounced these rules when he tried to pilfer some lobsters from a grocery store by, er, stuffing them down his shorts. As well as finding two live lobsters in his front pockets, police officers also found bags of shrimp and a pork loin tucked into the misguided man's waistband. He'd initially attempted to outrun the police, but tripped and fell. Delicious!

FAIL

'You know, everybody makes mistakes when they are president.'

Bill Clinton

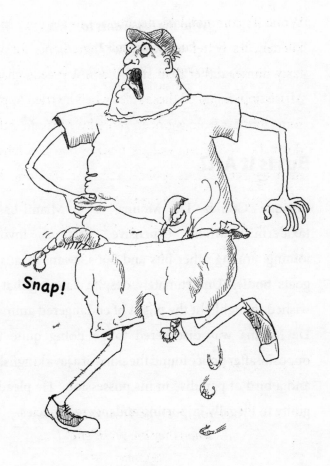

'Who the hell wants to
hear actors talk?'

Harry Warner of Warner Brothers
film studio, in 1927

But Is It Art?

Enrique Gomez De Molina is a Miami-based taxidermist whose expensive creations involve joining, among other bits and bobs, swans' heads to goats' bodies. Unfortunately, despite claiming that he wished to highlight the plight of endangered animals, De Molina was discovered to be doing quite the opposite after police found the skins of a Java kingfisher and a bird of paradise in his possession. He pleaded guilty to illegally importing endangered species.

Oh Deer!

If you get separated from your friend on a hunting trip, make sure he won't mistake you for the animal you're both meant to be shooting. Unfortunately one poor chap in Malaysia learned the hard way after he was shot by his friend, from whom he'd become separated, because his friend mistook him for a deer. The victim suffered wounds to his right thigh, chest, hand and cheek.

Hop, Skip and a . . . Bang!

In 1938 Major League baseball star Monty Stratton of the Chicago White Sox managed to end his own career while out hunting bunnies. Instead of shooting the floppy-eared darlings, the twenty-six-year-old accidentally shot himself in his (quite-useful-in-baseball) right leg. Worse still, after his injuries became infected with gangrene, his leg had to be amputated.

Man's Best Friend?

The prize for 'Most Humiliating Accidental Shooting Ever' goes to the duck-huntin' man from Utah who was shot in the bum by his own dog. The incident happened when the man and a friend were preparing for a morning's shoot on their boat. The soon-to-be victim of the unfortunate incident carefully laid down his gun to rest on the bottom of the boat and jumped into the water to set decoys for the ducks. His friend, meanwhile, manned the boat . . . but failed to man the dog, who got excited and started jumping around in the boat. Unfortunately he jumped right on top of the gun, shooting the decoy setter in the bottom. The dog's and ducks' bottoms were unharmed.

Clever Boy

You wait all your life to hear a funny story about a man being shot by his own dog, and then two come along at once. Billy E. Brown of Tampa, Florida, didn't see the funny side, however, when he was driving down a bumpy road with a pal on his way to hunt deer. With the car ready to go and fully loaded, which included placing his rifle pointing upwards between the two front seats, Brown's dog started to get a little overexcited and not only managed to knock the rifle towards his owner's right leg, but also to switch off the safety and pull the trigger. After being shot in the thigh, Brown was subsequently taken to hospital for surgery.

Game for Anything

Despite the British nation's fondness for game, some men have been known to take the eating of it a little too far. Not least an opportunistic man from the Isle of Wight, who was arrested after it was discovered he'd been shooting rooks and then selling them to a butcher. As wood pigeon is the only wild bird it's legal to sell for human consumption in the UK, the man was clearly breaking the law. The poor birds found a new home at a gastro-pub, where they ended up on the menu as 'rook salad'. The menu item was quickly removed; lots of people were told off.

> **'Gone With the Wind *is going to be the biggest flop in Hollywood history. I'm glad it'll be Clark Gable who's falling flat on his nose, not me.'***
>
> Actor Gary Cooper on turning down the role of Rhett Butler

Budgie Smuggler

A teenager in Scotland was electronically tagged for six months after being found literally smuggling budgies. Dean Wells tried to steal the small birds from his uncle's aviary but was caught red-handed. Wells was reportedly asked by his uncle what he was doing, to which he replied, 'I'm just looking at them'. But when police arrived to sort out the feathery debacle, Wells was found to have bulging pockets . . . which contained the two budgies.

Monkey Business

A drunk man from São Paulo got more than he bargained for when he entered an enclosure to 'play' with some monkeys. Arriving at Sorocaba Zoo rather the worse for wear, the nitwit climbed the fence and removed his top before wading through a pool to say 'hi' to some primates. Sadly the animals were not in the mood for larks, the spider monkeys repeatedly grabbing and biting the man in a rather nasty fashion. The monkey business finally came to an end when the intoxicated fool was dragged out of the pen by other zoo-goers. Not so much gorillas in the mist, then, as gorillas when you're pissed. (Sorry.)

The Eagle Has Landed

A Russian paraglider learned the hard way that no matter how experienced you might be at flying, you still can't account for birdlife. Flying high above the Himalayas, the poor soul's parachute was invaded by an eagle. Forced to make a dramatic landing in a tangle of rather unforgiving trees, the man can be seen in video footage swearing repeatedly as he struggles to disentangle the bird of prey. The eagle was reportedly released, unharmed, ten minutes after the Russian's inelegant landing.

FAIL

'Quite frankly, teachers are the only profession that teach our children.'

Dan Quayle

Snakes on a Plane

Smuggling snakes in a non-euphemistic way probably requires a bit of forward-planning, especially if you're trying to stash the snakes on a plane in your luggage. Sadly such preparation eluded an Iranian man, who was caught by customs having hidden snakes inside twenty-six of his socks. Unable to provide the authorities with documentation that explained his slithery cargo, the snake smuggler was handed over to the authorities for 'further interrogation', whereupon he no doubt found himself undergoing a thorough patting-down for his own 'snake' . . .

Safety First

While being kept awake by a barking dog can drive you mad, you should probably try to keep your cool if you're the sort of man who likes to keep his gun 'safe' under his pillow. As one man in Orange County, USA found out to his cost when the sound of a neighbour's dog barking in the wee hours provoked him to scrabble for his Colt Derringer. Unfortunately, in reaching for it, the irate man managed to shoot himself in the arm, while the dog escaped unharmed.

New Toy

After a lovely day drinking lots of lovely wine, Cambodian Kann Veasna found himself caught short and decided to have a furtive pee through a hole in a fence. What he didn't bargain for was the little yappy dog on the other side that mistook his manhood for a toy, and promptly bit it. Veasna was treated at a hospital for lacerations to his penis, with one doctor noting, 'It's undoubtedly sore now, but luckily it should still be useful to him in the future.'

'*The police are not here to create disorder;
they're here to preserve disorder.*'

Former Chicago mayor Richard M. Daley in 1968

Quick Pint?

When a German chap out on his horse decided to stop for a restorative pint of beer, little did he know it would turn into more than just the one drink. Upon leaving the pub some time later, the man realized he was really quite drunk and resolved to spend the rest of the night recuperating in an ATM vestibule. Discovered the next morning by a man in search of cash, the drunken German was found safe and well on the floor next to the thoroughly unimpressed horse.

FAIL

'It's not the pollution that's hurting the
environment; it's the impurities in our
air and water that are doing it.'

Dan Quayle

Only the Lonely

A German man felt so lonely he decided to cosy up to a 440 lb polar bear. Leaping into Knut the Bear's enclosure at Berlin Zoo, the thirty-year-old fool reportedly tried to 'make friends' with the predator, but was quickly dissuaded when zookeepers distracted the animal with meat and led it into a cage. The man allegedly told police that not only was he himself lonely, the bear too looked like it needed a friend. Awww.

FAIL

'This foreign-policy stuff is a little frustrating.'
George W. Bush

Duck!

In 1959 Harlow H. Curtice, the retired president of car manufacturer General Motors, managed to not merely harm but kill one of his best friends, Harry W. Anderson. While out hunting ducks in Walpole Island, USA the men's friendship came to an abrupt end when Anderson apparently took Curtice by surprise by standing up too suddenly, whereupon Curtice mistook him for a duck and shot him in the head.